THE
INFLUENCE
EDGE

THE
INFLUENCE
EDGE

How to
Persuade Others
to Help You
Achieve Your Goals

ALAN A. VENGEL

BK

BERRETT–KOEHLER PUBLISHERS, INC.

Berrett-Koehler Publishers, Inc.
235 Montgomery Street, Suite 650
San Francisco, CA 94104-2916
Tel: (415) 288-0260   Fax: (415) 362-2512   www.bkconnection.com

Ordering Information
Quantity sales. Special discounts are available on quantity purchases by corporations, associations, and others. For details, contact the "Special Sales Department" at the Berrett-Koehler address above.
Individual sales. Berrett-Koehler publications are available through most bookstores. They can also be ordered directly from Berrett-Koehler: Tel: (800) 929-2929; Fax: (802) 864-7626; www.bkconnection.com
Orders for college textbook/course adoption use. Please contact Berrett-Koehler: Tel: (800) 929-2929; Fax: (802) 864-7626.
Orders by U.S. trade bookstores and wholesalers. Please contact Ingram Publisher Services, Tel: (800) 509-4887; Fax: (800) 838-1149; E-mail: customer.service@ingrampublisherservices.com; or visit www.ingrampublisherservices.com/Ordering for details about electronic ordering.

Berrett-Koehler and the BK logo are registered trademarks of Berrett-Koehler Publishers, Inc.

Printed in the United States of America

Berrett-Koehler books are printed on long-lasting acid-free paper. When it is available, we choose paper that has been manufactured by environmentally responsible processes. These may include using trees grown in sustainable forests, incorporating recycled paper, minimizing chlorine in bleaching, or recycling the energy produced at the paper mill.

Library of Congress Cataloging-in-Publication Data

Vengel, Alan, 1947-
    The influence edge : how to persuade others to help you achieve your goals / Alan Vengel.
        p. cm.
    ISBN: 978-1-58376-156-4
    1. Teams in the workplace. I. Title.
    HD66 .V46 2000
    658.4'02—dc21   00-011285

First Edition
    12 11 10   14 13 12 11 10 9

Cover and Interior design and production: Susan Malikowski, Autographix

Table of Contents

Foreword

Every day here at Nortel Networks, people are asked to lead different projects. At times, we have employees working on three separate projects at the same time, with three separate workteams. Some of those team members might be right there beside their coworkers, while others are thousands of miles away, tied in through phone, fax, or email.

In spite of all the challenges of leading global teams, project leaders have got to work effectively with all the necessary players in order to successfully complete their assigned projects. Their success with one project is crucial because it determines what they are assigned next.

That doesn't sound so pathbreaking, you are probably thinking. And it's not—except that with hierarchies flattening everywhere at Nortel Networks, many times project leaders have to reach out laterally, using their own personal influence to forge the working relationships they need to get the job done right.

Now, that requires the much more challenging art of persuasion, or *influence*. And as organizations everywhere become flatter, and more web-like, being able to influence without direct authority grows ever more crucial—not just at Nortel Networks, but at companies around the world.

The Influence Edge™ has been taught here at Nortel Networks to dozens of employees. Many of these employees came away with a lifetime's worth of insightful practical strategies for persuading coworkers and business associates. Putting into practice The Influence Edge strategies was an important factor in meeting their project-related goals.

They have even attributed The Influence Edge strategies to helping them improve relationships not only at Nortel Networks but also with friends, family members, and spouses. No surprise—The Influence Edge is, after all, about tapping into what motivates people, what makes them move into action, what allows them to build good working relationships. It's a highly sophisticated technique built on the foundations of plain old human nature.

Now, Alan Vengel has taken the insights and skills that have long been available in his The Influence Edge workshops and put them together into one fun, easy-to-use workbook of the same name that works as well for individual readers as it does in small groups or across whole organizations. It's packed with worksheets, quick tip boxes, and funny and enlightening personal profiles based on people and situations Alan's actually dealt with in his career as an "influence" educator and consultant.

Now more than ever, you have to know how to get what you need from people. The old "I'm the boss!" style of influencing employees to do the job just isn't an option anymore in today's work environment. Thankfully *The Influence Edge* is available to highlight some great techniques. It continues to enhance the "networked" way we get things done here at Nortel Networks.

Angel Rampy
Manager, Nortel Networks

Introduction

How do you move people to action if you don't have direct authority—or even if you do have direct authority but don't care to exert it?

How do you get results from others without destroying relationships?

These are the questions I have addressed for over 20 years in conducting workshops on effective influence skills. They are the burning communication questions of managers and professionals in every organization where I have consulted.

One thing is clear: the ability to influence people is not something you must be born with, but something anyone can learn. That is why I have written *The Influence Edge*. It's a precise system of behavioral skills that you can use over and over again, to move others to action at work, in personal relationships, and in everyday life. In fact, my Influence Edge workshop materials have been used successfully in hundreds of organizations all over the world.

Now I have taken highlights from The Influence Edge workshop materials and put them into this fun and easy-to-use workbook full of strategies you can learn quickly and put to use immediately. It will help you get started turning the often disorderly and difficult task of getting someone else to help you achieve your goals into an entirely viable process of analysis, preparation, and action. Just follow the system presented on the following pages, practice some of the short exercises, and you are on your way. You will not only be better prepared for those difficult situations, you will also build productive relationships and get more done in less time.

I start in Chapter One by showing you how and why the ability to influence others is essential to getting work done. Chapters Two, Three, and Four introduce you to a powerful system of influence behaviors and strategic thinking. Chapters Five and Six describe the nuts and bolts of planning for a real influence situation and how to map out your strategy. And finally, Chapter Seven goes deeper into the practice of influence to show you how to build a better long-term rapport with really difficult people.

When it comes to getting other people to get the job done, nothing succeeds like the art of influence. This workbook is your starter kit. If you are interested in the complete The Influence Edge program for yourself or your organization, contact me at:

Alan Vengel
Vengel Consulting Group, Inc.
1230 Dutch Mill Drive
Danville, CA 94526
Tel: 925/837-0148
E-mail: VCG@vengelconsulting.com

CHAPTER ONE

Why You Need Influence Skills

Let's start by looking at a few situations that I see and hear about all the time in my role as an influence skills-building consultant.

- Yolanda is the head of Human Resources at FactPoint, a mid-sized communications company. She's working on deadline to put together a new employee handbook, but she's stuck on one section because one of the company's vice presidents won't get her the documentation she needs to complete it. She has already put in several requests. Clearly, getting her the information is not the vice president's highest priority, but Yolanda needs it as soon as possible. How can she get the information she needs?

- Gary, a brand management director for a large food packager, has a great new marketing idea for a languishing line of cereals, but it's a bit experimental and he has

If It Were Only That Easy

Recently, at a workshop at a major Bay Area geo-tech company, a scientist approached me on the first break of the morning.

"Why," she said, "do we have to do this influence stuff? Can't people just do the work like they're supposed to?"

This was not the first time I had heard this question from someone recently promoted to a management position. People such as this scientist enthusiastically sign up for the work to do whatever their specialty is, but once promoted to team leader, all that changes.

"In a perfect world," I told her, "yes, everyone would do the work as you need it done. But this is not a perfect world and everyone sees it differently. That's why you've got to see the world from their point of view, and then get them to do the same—to make your priorities theirs.

"Hence, the need to influence . . . and to influence well!"

no way of proving to senior management that it will definitely raise sales. In other words, their approval would have to be at least in part an act of faith. How does he get them to green-light a budget and staff for his brainchild?

- Vera has designed and implemented a collaborative performance-feedback process for the department she heads at CompuStar, a mid-size Silicon Valley firm. The process has vastly improved communication, efficiency, and productivity, and she knows other department heads would benefit from it if they would give it a try. But she's no vice president, just one department head among many. How does she get the other department heads to open up to her idea?

- Roberto, sales director for a series of mail-order catalogs, has thought up a whole new sales campaign and needs the expertise of a certain consulting firm his company has worked with in the past to put it into action. But this time around, he doesn't have the money in his budget to afford the firm's expensive services. How can he get the firm's input when he can't afford to hire them?

For Yolanda, Gary, Vera, and Roberto, their solution lies in two simple words: influence skills. Let's face it—the workplace isn't what it used to be. Organizations are getting flatter, more collaborative, and team-oriented in their decision-making, and less overtly dependent on a clear chain of command from top to bottom. That means that old-fashioned, crack-the-whip authority doesn't carry the weight it once did.

Even if you still have the chance to bark out orders and edicts left and right, it's simply not the most effective way anymore of getting what you want from people. Workers, like all human beings, thrive on a sense of being needed and appreciated, of having a shared stake in something. They *don't* thrive on demands and threats from on-high.

Influence skills are even *more* important if you don't have clear authority. Since most of the time we don't have clear authority, influence skills as presented in this workbook are designed to help everyone, from bosses dealing with people reporting to them to people reporting to bosses—not to mention the colleagues, suppliers, vendors, customers, clients, team members, contractors, and even competitors we all have to deal with every day. *To be successful, we must have the ability to influence people over whom we have no direct control.* Learning effective influence skills to win the willing commitment of others gives us the edge we need to get what we want and build more productive business relationships—even when we have the so-called authority to enforce rather than cultivate compliance. *Especially* when we have the authority to enforce compliance.

Take a moment to fill out Worksheet 1, which gets you to think about where you want to have more influence in your life.

Determining Where You Want More Influence

Take a moment to think about your life. In what areas do you want more influence?

WORK AREAS

Upper Management: what would you want to influence them about?

_____

_____

Peers: what would you want to influence them about?

_____

_____

Support Groups: what would you want to influence them about?

_____

_____

PERSONAL AREAS

Family: what would you want to influence them about?

_____

_____

Friends: what would you want to influence them about?

_____

_____

Others: what would you want to influence them about?

_____

_____

The Importance of Influence in the 21st Century Workplace

While I was interviewing a manager in a high-tech manufacturing company to help her customize a program, the following exchange took place:

"We're matrixed," the manager stated, "so no one works for anyone and everyone reports to everyone. Decisions require support, and anyone with more information than you has power. We exert influence across all organizational boundaries, and informal support can make or break a project."

"What kinds of skills do your people need?" I asked.

"They need to plan for every meeting with the same attention to detail they would apply to their technical projects. You can't ignore the people side of a project. People are the reason why a project will succeed or fail. Give me people who can compete for resources without burning the relationship and I'll hire them."

At this point you're probably thinking, *so it's better to use influence with people rather than Authority.* But what's the difference between influence and manipulation?

Effective influence focuses not just on getting us what we need or want, but on improving the relationship. Thus, we are honest and sincere about our objectives, flexible in our approach, and aware that the people we are dealing with have their own goals or priorities. Manipulation, on the other hand, uses the relationship only to accomplish what we want with little or no consideration of the impact on the other person. Call it the "hit and run" approach if you will.

FIVE GOOD REASONS FOR ATTAINING INFLUENCE SKILLS . . . NO MATTER WHAT YOU DO!

1. Old-fashioned formal authority just doesn't cut it anymore. Organizations are flatter, work is done more as a team effort, and everyone has a say. Direct control over others is limited.
2. Your ability to influence is directly related to your individual success at work.
3. It's more important than ever to approach situations with both a thought-out plan and the flexibility to adapt it to meet others' needs as well as your own.
4. In our flatter work world, it's more expected than ever that you should know how to work with other people so that everyone's goals are met.
5. Well-honed influence skills help you:
   - Get work done faster.
   - Reduce conflict.
   - Relieve stress.
   - Demonstrate that you are a team player.
   - Be a better negotiator.

Determining What You Know About Influence

You have influenced and been influenced your entire life. It's important to identify how you have been influenced, what works on you, and what does not work on you.

BEST	WORST
Who are some of the best influencers you have run across? What have they done?	Who are some of the worst influencers you have run across? What have they done?
_____	_____
_____	_____
_____	_____
What impact on you will future dealings with this person have?	What impact on you will future dealings with this person have?
_____	_____
_____	_____
_____	_____

Building Your Strategy

These typical influence-based situations may sound as familiar to you as they would to Yolanda, Gary, Vera, and Roberto, our model influencers:

- You need someone to provide you with necessary information so that you can accomplish your goal. Giving you the information is not the other person's highest priority.
- You need to get support from senior management for a new project. The support could be in the form of money or a headcount.
- You have made some time saving and money saving improvements in your department and you would like to influence managers in other parts of your organization to make the same improvements.
- You need the help of an expert who has more experience than you in a certain task, but that person is very, very busy.
- You have explained to someone what you need or want in a logical, rational way. You have even used data to back up your position. But the other person resists seeing your point or helping you out.

Take a moment to think of other situations you have heard about or experienced where the ability to influence someone was key to your getting what you needed. Then take a look at Worksheet 3, which gets you to assess what it is you most need in situations where you need to influence someone. Is it to sell your ideas, to get support for a project, to build a better working relationship? Use Worksheet 3 to think about how influence skills would most benefit your life. You will be referring back to Worksheet 3 in later exercises and worksheets as you apply the influence skills you will learn here to challenges in your own life.

Focusing Your Influence Needs

Determine which three of the nine areas below are most important to you. Place a 1, 2, or 3 in the box to the right reflecting your first, second, and third priorities. You will want to keep all three of your selections in mind as you work through this book—and pay specific attention to your first priority.

Generally, how would you want to improve? What would you like more effective influence to help you do?

1. To sell my ideas better . . . . □

2. To get support for my projects . . . . □

3. To build rapport and better relationships . . . . □

4. To be more savvy in political situations . . . . □

5. To run more effective meetings . . . . □

6. To be more flexible in tough situations . . . . □

7. To get people more involved and committed . . . . □

8. To handle conflict more effectively in both business and personal life . . . □

9. To be able to read people and situations more effectively . . . . □

Identifying a Specific Influence Situation

Now, identify a current situation in your life where applying what you learn in this workbook will help you increase your influence ability. Take your time in choosing because you will be referring back to this situation throughout the workbook, and you will have a surefire influence plan for it by the end.

SITUATION:

Who do you want to influence? _____

What do you want to influence them about?

_____

_____

_____

_____

What are the challenges you face in this situation?

_____

_____

_____

_____

What is your time frame? Do you have just one meeting to influence? Or an option for several meetings?

_____

_____

_____

_____

CHAPTER TWO

Mastering the Two Fundamental Factors of Any Influence Situation

Knowing what you want or need from people isn't enough to help you influence successfully—you have to know what *they* want. You also have to have some sense of the pressures and priorities within their own department or organization so you can take that into account when approaching them. In this chapter, you will learn how to prepare to meet your influence subject by thinking through not only your own needs and goals but what the other person's might be as well. Later you will learn how to tailor your influence strategy to *both* sides of the influence fence.

Breaking down an influence situation into the two fundamental factors—Your Goal and The Other Person—will

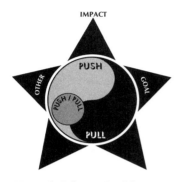

Figure 1. Influence Model

help you be able to anticipate the reaction of your influence subject and sort out how best to proceed, even when you've only got minutes to do it.

Before analyzing a situation, take a moment to think about yourself in relation to the other person and his situation. Put yourself in your subject's shoes and listen to your own words of persuasion as though you have never heard them before. To better visualize your influence situation, examine Figure 1 on the left.

THE TWO FUNDAMENTAL FACTORS OF ANY INFLUENCE SITUATION

Your Goal

- What do I want?
- What will make it clear to the other person?
- What assumptions am I making about the person(s) I need to influence?

The Other Person(s)

- What is their mindset?
- What is important to them?
- What is going on in their organization or department that might affect the situation?

JIM'S STORY

Of all the product developers at PraxisWare, an up-and-coming software maker, no one knows the products better, has built such good rapport with key customers, or has recruited as many talented coworkers as Jim Casey. For that reason, Jim's boss, Sharon Grander, has recently chosen him to head up a major new software development project that could be the company's breakthrough contribution to the market. She's backed him with all the resources he needs and the proper budget, and PraxisWare's largest customer has already expressed interest in the product application that he and his team have developed. All he needs now is to move into the critical Stage Two phase of product development testing, so the product can be brought to market as soon as possible.

Unfortunately, Ed Hanson, the senior engineering manager, is standing squarely in the way of the necessary testing for Stage Two completion and product roll-out. Because he's responsible for keeping product quality testing for the whole company moving along, he says he "doesn't have time to fiddle around with something that is not proven." In other words, he wants Jim to get in line with the rest of the new product developers and wait his turn. Meanwhile, important members of Jim's team are getting restless, saying that if this project is stalled much longer, they want to go on to something that doesn't have Ed Hanson as a road block.

Jim desperately needs to convince Ed of the importance of beginning testing immediately. He has a strong feeling Ed's main objection is that testing immediately may open the flood gates for all the project managers to demand special attention for their "pet projects"—not to mention Ed doesn't seem convinced that Jim's new application can be the breakthrough seller for PraxisWare that Jim is certain it will be from the Stage One test results.

How can Jim get Ed to share his conviction that the new product merits special attention so it can go to market immediately and satisfy that impatient major customer? How does he get Ed on his side?

Jim's Dilemma

Understand your situation; be prepared for all possible issues. Respond to the following questions concerning Jim's impending confrontation with Ed.

1. What are the main issues likely to emerge in this upcoming meeting (interpersonal, organizational, etc.)?

_____

_____

_____

2. Which of these issues do you believe will be the top two or three that must be resolved by the end of the meeting?

_____

_____

_____

 ## A Minute of Your Time

Now, keeping the two fundamental factors in mind, take a minute to consider Jim Casey's situation with Ed Hanson. What is Jim's goal? What do you think is important to Ed? What is Ed looking for from Jim?

A CLOSER LOOK AT THE TWO FUNDAMENTAL FACTORS

1. Your Goal

What do you want? What will make it clear to the other person?

You have probably heard the saying, "If you don't know what you want, anything will do." If you want a better chance of getting what you want, you have to determine your goal and think about how you can communicate it effectively to the other person. You need to figure out specifically what you want the other person to say or do. Here is how to determine your goal:

- Think about whom you need to influence. Sometimes, the first person who comes to mind is not really the person we need to influence.
- Give yourself a time frame so you can communicate your need to the other person.
- A good way to determine if you have a specific goal is to ask yourself, "How will I know when I reach my goal? What will the other person have done for me?" Be very clear and specific with the person, such as "I thought you could get this information for me by setting up a phone interview with your vice president of research."
- State the goal in positive terms. It's not what you want them to stop doing, but rather to begin doing.
- Is there someone else to influence before or concurrently with your influence subject?

Now ask yourself, *What is my mindset?*

Influence is a very specific form of communication—you have to consider your mindset as well as the mindset of the other person. When thinking about your own mindset, check any assumptions that you are making about the other person and about the situation. Are you making assumptions about who has power, personal investment, the level of trust, or your level of expertise? Here is how to find out:

- Look at the situation as objectively as possible.
- Increase your power in the situation by determining ways the other person needs you.
- Find someone who has been successful influencing others in a similar situation and ask that person for ideas on how you might proceed.

2. The Other Person(s)

What is the mindset of your influence subject(s)? What is important to them?

Now it's time to put yourself in the other person's shoes. How might he view you and your motives? From his perspective, who has the power? Does the other person trust your intentions? How valuable to the other person is his relationship with you? Do you think the other person respects and trusts your expertise and what you bring to the proposal? Here is how to find out:

- Think about what you could do to make it easier for the other person to go along with you and agree with your goal.
- Put yourself in the other person's shoes. How would you respond to being influenced in this situation? Why?
- Try to get a sense of the other person's mindset from people familiar with the situation. What is their history with the other person? What types of proposals have won the other person's approval in other situations?
- What is going on in the other person's organization? What does the organization's history, or the other person's history within the organization, suggest about the present?

A Minute of Your Time

Go back to Jim's story. Consider what Jim's goal might be. What assumptions will he be making about the situation? What do you think is important to Ed? What is Ed looking for from Jim? What departmental factors come into play in his thinking and/or willingness to cooperate with Jim?

Applying the Two Fundamental Factors

Go back to your own influence situation that you outlined in Worksheet 4 and break it down into the two fundamental factors.

1. Write down your influence goal. What do you want in this situation, and what will make it clear to the other person? What assumptions are you making about the other person?

_____

_____

_____

_____

_____

2. Write down your take on the other person's point of view. What is important to them? What isn't? What has worked with them before?

_____

_____

_____

_____

_____

If you have only a few minutes to assess an influence situation before you take action, breaking it down into these two fundamental factors is the fastest way to get a handle on the situation and craft a strategy before plunging in. You will learn how to strategize with expert precision when you apply the two factors and the behavior models you will master in the next chapter.

INFLUENCING A GROUP

A question I am often asked in this increasingly team-driven age of work concerns dealing with groups of people. What do you do when you have to influence not only one person but a whole team or group? The strategies you will learn in this workbook are just as valuable for dealing with people in a team situation as dealing with people on a one-on-one basis. Teams are made up of many personalities, motives, and agendas—some explicit, some hidden. As the influencer, you don't want to be blind-sided by unexpected factors, so, first and foremost, try to learn as much as possible about your target team or group before you formally approach them. Find out who the "key stakeholders" are and try to talk to them and feel them out before you meet with the whole group.

Some other pointers for influencing a group:

- Break the group apart in your mind and make some educated guesses about what the group members' conflicting agendas might be.

- Be clear on what you want from the group as a result of this meeting. What is your call to action? Also, don't hesitate to make an emotional appeal as well as a rational one if it is at all appropriate.

- If possible, form a coalition with those in the group with whom you have the most common ground, either around goals and values or fears and concerns. Do this before the meeting, if possible. Be prepared to capitalize on this common ground during the meeting.

- Make sure you provide both a well-researched and thought-out rationale for your argument and a clear vision of how it will lead to future success.

Influencing a Group

You may find yourself on more than one team or you may find your team must influence other teams. To do this most strategically you would want to identify the key stakeholders in each group. The key stakeholders are those people who are most important to helping you get what you want. Fill out this worksheet to help you determine what you want from a team on which you currently serve and from the other teams linked to it.

IDENTIFY THE KEY STAKEHOLDERS IN THE TEAMS BELOW:

Upper Management Team

Stakeholder #1 _____

Stakeholder #2 _____

Your Team

Stakeholder #1 _____

Stakeholder #2 _____

YOU

Support Team

Stakeholder #1 _____

Stakeholder #2 _____

Team Two

Stakeholder #1 _____

Stakeholder #2 _____

Eventually the successful influencer will develop strategies to approach and influence all the important stakeholders in the situation.

Now go on to the related Worksheet 8.

27

Determining Your Action Steps

Using the names that appear on Worksheet 7, answer the following questions.

Which stakeholders do I need to get to know better?

_____

_____

_____

_____

_____

How will I do this?

_____

_____

_____

_____

_____

How will influencing this stakeholder affect my situation?

_____

_____

_____

_____

_____

CHAPTER THREE

Learning the Key Behaviors That Drive Influence Success

We have established that there are two fundamental factors to any influence situation. This fairly simple principle becomes complicated, however, when we communicate with at least one other person within an influence situation. This communication produces a certain *energy*. Think about it. Haven't you ever felt someone making a real effort to impress upon you the necessity or urgency of doing something? That's Push energy. Or haven't you ever felt really drawn to people or their ideas because they showed they really understood your point of view? That's Pull energy. Put them together, as we often do in trying to influence people, and you get Push/Pull energy. Knowing how to harness these two energies is the key that drives this influence model.

Before we go on, let's take another look at our influence model represented by Figure 1 on the next page.

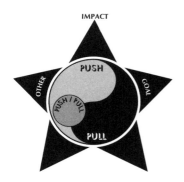

Figure 1. Influence Model

As you can see, the two fundamental factors—Your Goal and The Other Person—are clearly identifiable in the figure. But in the middle, represented by the classic Asian symbol of *yin and yang* (meaning two opposite forces that complement each other), you will notice the words Push and Pull—two fundamentally different yet often complementary influence energies that interact with the two fundamental factors. Now let's look at these two energies a little more closely.

WHAT IS PUSH ENERGY?

Push energy is direct, forceful, and persuasive. It's not being aggressive so much as it is being *assertive*, or offering specific suggestions. It moves against people's inclinations to get them to change course or initiate action. They may resist, withdraw, or even push back, but if you know how and when to use Push energy effectively, it can yield amazing results. For example:

Some restaurant patrons state their desires clearly: "I want a steak, medium rare, pare off the fat, baked potato with butter, no sour cream, string beans, and a very dry martini straight up. And I need to be out of here in 30 minutes." They know exactly what they want and how they want it. You don't need to read their minds or clarify details with them, and they definitely are not asking for your input or advice.

Some meeting managers also state their desires clearly: "I need to submit by the middle of next week a report to the Webmaster I've hired on what we want our Website to contain. So I'm breaking you up into ten different teams that'll each meet from 2-4 p.m. today and tomorrow, and by 5 p.m. Friday I need each team to submit their responses to this worksheet I've created on what you think our site should include. I want each team to fill out the whole sheet, and if there are questions or concerns, I'll appoint each team a representative to take those issues straight to me."

Figure 2. Push Energy

Being Smart About Push Energy

How comfortable are you when people use Push energy with you?
Rate yourself below.

	Not at All			Somewhat. Depends on How It's Used				Very Comfortable. I Prefer It	
1	2	3	4	5	6	7	8	9	10

When does Push energy work with you? When does it fail?

_____

_____

_____

_____

Can you think of a recent situation in which someone used Push energy with you?
What did it feel like? Did it work?

_____

_____

_____

_____

You will look at your own skills with Push energy in just a moment.

Figure 3. Pull Energy

WHAT IS PULL ENERGY?

Pull energy is inclusive and involving. It requires listening attentively and asking questions to *draw others out* and engage them. Pull energy moves *with* other people to help them see alternatives, and encourages their engagement by showing a greater understanding of their issues and needs. It may seem "soft" at times, but when used correctly, it can help gain commitment, break down resistance, and create and support strong, productive relationships between people.

For example: Sally Pullwell, one of your work colleagues, wants to get you involved on an account you are not sure you have time for. So instead of asking you outright to share the load, Sally takes you out to your favorite Thai restaurant for lunch and "picks your brain" on the matter by asking you lots of open-ended questions. "I mean, how would *you* go about developing this account?" she asks. The more you talk about it, the more interested you become. She doesn't have to ask directly because you already feel involved, and before you know it, you are her co-director. Now how did *that* happen?

When you say, "Sally, I just don't have the time to make an open commitment to this account," Sally says, "Okay, it sounds like you are really busy, so let's make this short. How do you think I should approach this project? Could I get someone for one afternoon a week? If you were on a project like this, what kind of people would you get? If we could reduce the workload to one afternoon a week, would that be enough to get you on board?" It's much harder to dismiss a focused request like this, with carefully defined parameters, than an open, and seemingly limitless, call for help.

Your colleague Jack Greenleaf wants you to undertake a new project with him, but you don't think your mutual boss, Roz Jefferson, will give either of you the support you need.

Jack trusts you enough to reveal: "Well, actually, Roz said she'd rather I work with you on the project because of your experience, but if you weren't interested I should ask who you might recommend." "Roz really said *that?*" you ask in reply. Jack seems sincere and he is showing trust by sharing this information with you. "How should we ask Roz for the kind of support we'll need?" he asks.

Pull Energy Is Smart Strategy

A senior manager at a fast-moving software company approached me with the following question: "My people are smart, fast, and young. They like money, but how else can I motivate them?"

Here is what I told her. "If the money you're offering is equal to the industry norms, then think about motivating your best people by understanding them better. Using Pull behaviors like listening, asking open-ended questions and asking focused questions all help you know your talent, their needs, and their passions. That way," I told her, "you can assign and design the best learning and development situations.

"This is the key to keeping these talented people challenged."

Being Smart About Pull Energy

How comfortable are you when people use Pull energy with you?
Rate yourself below.

	Not at All			Somewhat. Depends on How It's Used				Very Comfortable. I Prefer It		
1	2	3	4	5	6	7	8	9	10

When does Pull energy work with you? When does it fail?

_____

_____

_____

_____

Can you think of a recent situation in which someone used Pull energy with you?
What did it feel like? Did it work?

_____

_____

_____

_____

You will look at your own skills with Pull energy in just a moment.

Figure 4. Push/Pull Energy

WHAT IS PUSH/PULL ENERGY?

Push/Pull energy is a blend of the best of both Push and Pull energy, meant for those times when it's appropriate to be not only direct and forceful but also inclusive, motivational, and considerate of the other person. It can also have a dual impact. For example, even as your boss Roz pushes you into the project with Jack, she also pulls you in with a rosy picture of how you will be rewarded. The impact on you is that you may feel pushed but also pulled.

For example: Roz calls you into her office later in the day. "Listen, I know you're overworked right now, but if you take on this extra project with Jack, I'll cut out about half your administrative responsibilities. This way you can really devote the best part of your brain to the project. It's a chance for you to be really working at your highest level."

Or it could go like this. Roz leans forward at her desk, tells you to shut the door, and says, "Listen, if you will consider working with Jack and taking this idea successfully to market, I will give you first crack at the next research and development project that comes along. I know this is where your interests lie, and I will commit to making it happen for you."

Being Smart About Push/Pull Energy

How comfortable are you when people use Push/Pull energy with you?
Rate yourself below.

Not at All				Somewhat. Depends on How It's Used				Very Comfortable. I Prefer It		
1	2	3	4	5	6	7	8	9	10

When does Push/Pull energy work with you? When does it fail?

_____

_____

_____

_____

Can you think of a recent situation in which someone used Push/Pull energy with you? What did it feel like? Did it work?

_____

_____

_____

_____

You will look at your own skills with Push/Pull energy in just a moment.

THE FIVE KEY BEHAVIORS OF PUSH, PULL, AND PUSH/PULL ENERGY

Now I'm going to introduce you to the five essential behaviors that make up Push, Pull, and Push/Pull energy. These five key behaviors are essential and will give you a "quickstart" to the influence process, one that you can use immediately.

First, Push behaviors. Push behaviors state your position and get your point across directly. They have a "one way" feeling, a sense of clarity, purpose, and persistence. They result in clear action, logical conclusions, and an understanding of the impact of the request. They are based on clearly stated goals and logical reasons. You are using Push behaviors when you:

1. Assert (clearly and directly what you want).
2. Suggest (concrete ways the other person can help you get it).

Pull behaviors, on the other hand, draw the other person out through questions and active listening. They help you understand the other person's position and create shared commitment. They promote greater inclusion and openness and lead to increased rapport, understanding, and commitment. You are using Pull behaviors when you:

3. Ask Questions

There are two kinds of questions you can ask. "Open-ended questions" gather information and find out what the other person is thinking. "Focused questions" help the other person focus on alternatives. A related kind of Pull behavior is to:

4. Summarize (back what the person has said so you can clarify issues and demonstrate understanding).

And finally, Push/Pull behaviors both provide direction/clarity and promote agreement and commitment. A blend of Push and Pull behaviors, they are all too often overlooked, but successful influencers recognize their power. For example, you are using Push/Pull behaviors when you:

5. Offer Incentives (making it easier or more attractive for the other person to do what you are asking).

Use Push behaviors when you:
- know what you want.
- have good reasons with which to build a case.
- believe you need to take a more direct approach.

Use Pull behaviors when you:
- want to build a relationship with the other person.
- need the commitment and involvement of others.
- require additional information to help achieve your goals.

Use Push/Pull behaviors when you want to:
- create breakthrough results.
- provide meaningful exchanges.

⚒ Building Your Strategy

Now, let's assess your current proficiency. Take the below self-quiz on the five behaviors just described. As you go through each area, think back to situations where you needed to influence others. Determine if you would like to use each behavior:

1) less often
2) about the same
3) more often
4) differently

Place the appropriate number in the column to the right of each behavior. You might want to use two numbers: 1 and 4, for example, meaning that you would like to use the behavior less often, but also that when you do use it, you use it differently.

PUSH

1. Assert (clearly and directly what you want) ___ ___
2. Suggest (concrete ways the other person
   can help you get it) ___ ___

PULL

3. Ask Questions (both open-ended and focused) ___ ___
4. Summarize (back what the person has said
   so you can clarify issues and demonstrate
   understanding) ___ ___

PUSH/PULL

5. Offer Incentives (making it easier or more
   attractive for the other person to do what
   you are asking) ___ ___

Self-Assessment

Are you more comfortable with Push behaviors or Pull behaviors? Why?

_____

_____

_____

_____

Any patterns that you notice? Where would you like to improve?

_____

_____

_____

_____

Select one behavior—Push, Pull, or Push/Pull—that seems most important for you to improve upon. Why this one?

_____

_____

_____

If you were to use this behavior more effectively, what impression would you leave on others?

_____

_____

_____

_____

PUTTING THE FIVE KEY BEHAVIORS TO WORK FOR YOU

Now let's consider the Push behavior you said you may want to improve. Think of a situation in your life where you'd like to use it more often, or better. What might your opening lines be? And how might the behavior backfire if you overuse it?

Let's take the Assert behavior, for instance.

Your opening lines might start with:

- "I need . . ." (then continue with: ". . . two more weeks to perfect this marketing plan.")
- "I want . . ." (then continue with: ". . . two more staffers on this project to complete it effectively.")
- "I should have . . ." (then continue with: ". . . a new sports utility vehicle if I'm going to be chauffeuring three kids and their friends around town all day.")

But if you Assert too much without varying your influence strategies, you:

- may seem too pushy.
- may not get commitment or build rapport.

What if it were a Pull behavior you said you'd like to improve? As an example, let's use the Ask Questions behavior. Your discourse in this case might begin with:

- "How should we . . ." (then continue with: ". . . structure this deal based on your past experiences?")
- "What do you think about . . ." (then continue with: ". . . setting up a satellite office in Portland to deal with West Coast sales?")
- "What concerns you about . . ." (then continue with: ". . . making our products available to customers through an on-line catalog?")

But if you Ask Questions too often, you might:

- seem as though you have no valuable information, firm opinion, or clear position on the issues.

Okay, now look at the Push/Pull behavior you may want to improve. For the behavior Offer Incentives, you might start off with:

- "If you . . ." (then continue with: ". . . sit in for me at that development meeting.")
- "I will . . ." (then continue with: ". . . take those obnoxious clients from Pittsburgh to lunch for you tomorrow.")
- "Here's what I can do for you . . ." (then continue with: ". . . give you a 10% cut of all profits from the project in addition to the salary I've offered you—if you'll agree to supervise it.")
- "In exchange, I will . . ." (then continue with: ". . . take the kids to soccer practice on Saturday morning so you can sleep in—*if* I get that sports utility vehicle, that is.")

But Offer Incentives too often, and you:

- may been seen as trying to solve issues too quickly.
- may overlook important differences in where you and the other person are coming from.
- may be seen as someone who thinks she can get what she wants through "buying" people, or bribery.

⚒ Building Your Strategy

Now that you have come up with opening lines for each of the behaviors you would like to use more effectively or more often, take a few minutes to brainstorm where, how, and with whom you can use them, and what it might sound like. Start with low-threshold situations and work your way up to friends, family members, and work associates.

For example, if your chosen Push behavior was Assert, you could start using assertive language in a restaurant:

"I want a cheeseburger, medium rare, with cheddar cheese and a jumbo order of fries. And I need to be at a meeting in 45 minutes."

instead of:

"Um, would it be okay if I had, like a cheeseburger? Like, with fries? Okay?"

From there, you might feel ready to practice assertive language in a family or work context:

"I need to have a 2,000-word proposal for this project by Friday afternoon before 3 p.m."

instead of:

"Well, I guess I'd like to have a proposal by the end of the week . . . maybe Friday?"

If your chosen Pull behavior was Ask Questions, you could start doing so in a store:

"What do you think would be a nice gift for a couple that just gave birth to octuplets?"

instead of:

"I need you to pick out a present for my friends who just had eight kids, and it better not be too expensive."

From there, you might feel ready to practice this behavior in a work context:

"Given the internal politics involved, what do you think is the smartest way to market and promote this new service?"

instead of:

"I've already come up with a total marketing plan for this new service, and I need you to work on it. Your responsibilities are on page 32. Read it over the weekend and start in on Monday."

If you chose to improve your use of the Push/Pull behavior Offer Incentives, you could start doing so with your home newspaper delivery person:

"If you deliver the paper to the side entrance of the house instead of the front, I'll write a letter to your manager about the great service you are providing."

instead of:

"I'm gonna report to the circulation manager that the paper is always getting stuck in the front bushes."

From there, you might feel ready to practice this behavior in a work context:

"If you loan me two good technicians from your department for this project, here's what I can do for you: help you put together a proposal for your idea about introducing R&D brainstorming days for your staff."

Pull Energy in Action

Meg, one of my former students, called me on the phone needing advice on a situation with her boss. It seems the boss was reluctant to let her attend a three-day seminar at a major professional conference. Meg viewed this reluctance on his part as a signal that he wasn't interested in her personal development.

"Does this mean I should move on to another job?" she asked me.

For starters, I wanted to help her see that she did not have enough facts to know her boss's motivations for not letting her go, and that she was making a giant assumption that needed to be checked out. Secondly, I told her she needed to put herself in her boss's position. How would *she* respond if one of *her* people approached her with a request to spend time away?

It became clear that she needed to ask her boss both *open-ended* and *focused* questions to begin developing an effective approach. Sure enough, when she went back to her boss with some questions, he explained that he had denied her request to go to the conference because he needed a way to cover for her while she was away. Together, they negotiated a solution and Meg got to go to the conference after all.

In the case of Meg and her boss, her questioning Pull behaviors opened up a conversation and led to a new level of understanding between the two.

Practicing in the Field

Complete this worksheet once you have had a few days to practice your behaviors in a real life setting, whether that's at home, at a restaurant or store, or with clients at the workplace.

What behaviors have you consciously tried in the past day or two?

_____

_____

What has been the result? What worked? What did not?

_____

_____

How did your subject respond?

_____

_____

How did you personally feel using each of your chosen behaviors?

_____

_____

How will you practice with them further?

_____

_____

CHAPTER FOUR

Attuning to Personal Communication Styles

By this point, you have already learned some valuable tools for getting people to come around to your point of view. Not only have you learned how to do a quick but useful assessment of the two fundamental factors of any influence situation (your goal and your influence subject), you have also learned five different behavioral approaches, which of the five you are already versed in, which of the five you need to work on, and how to apply them to situations in and out of the workplace. Now you are going to learn another strategy—not just *what* to say to your influence subjects to break through to their own wants and needs, but *how* to say it in a way that is attuned to their personal communication styles. The Four Communication Styles you need to be aware of are: the Authoritarian, the Analyzer, the Visionary, and the Supporter.

But first, take a minute to think about what you wrote down under The Other Person when you were breaking down the two fundamental factors for your own personal influence situation. What did you speculate was your subject's mindset? What did you think was important to her? Take a moment to fill out Worksheet 14 to help re-familiarize yourself with your personal influence situation.

Revisiting Your Situation

Situation (should be current and something coming up in the next week or two):

_____

_____

_____

_____

Identify your subject (the person most important for you to influence):

_____

Identify what you want from your subject (cooperation, information, connections, etc.):

_____

_____

_____

_____

Now ask yourself another question about your subject: what kind of communicator is he? How do you believe your subject wants to be approached or responded to?

Why do I ask? Because having a sense of your subject's communication style can provide valuable help in choosing which influence behaviors will be most effective. The following four classic communication styles have long served to help me and my clients get a handle on their influence subjects and put together a more focused, powerful influence strategy.

Authoritarians We Have Known

One of my clients, Ben, a human resources representative at a major computer manufacturer was frustrated with a new manager who had joined his business unit. The new manager seemed overly forceful and at times aggressive when dealing with Ben, uncooperative and short with him in staff meetings.

"How should I deal with this manager?" Ben asked me. "I tried to engage him by asking open-ended questions and using listening skills, but he just gets annoyed and wants to move away from me."

I suggested that Ben change his approach from the Pull behaviors he was using to Push behaviors—that he be more direct and assertive, adopting the new manager's own personal style. If appropriate, he might even offer the new manager an incentive of some sort for communicating constructively with him. I also suggested that Ben possibly ask the new manager how he wanted to be approached.

THE AUTHORITARIAN:

- prefers to be in control.
- makes decisions quickly.
- focuses on the task at hand.
- is fast-paced.
- prefers brief, well-organized communication.
- wants to be in charge.

We have all worked with—or for—at least one Authoritarian, and we know they can be as brusque and intimidating as they are clear-spoken and, very often, highly effective. They don't like to get bogged down in details. They believe in structure. They are usually interested in the bottom line (meaning the end results, financial or otherwise). They come across as active and confident, if perhaps a bit arrogant, and sometimes they may act without taking into account all the relevant facts, or considering the impact of their decision on other people.

Authoritarians are likely to say things like:
- "What's the bottom line?"
- "Get to the point."
- "Put it in a memo!"

The Authoritarian and You

What is your reaction to an authoritarian style of communication? Who do you know who uses this style?

_____

_____

_____

_____

Do you need to change your reaction to this style?

_____

_____

_____

_____

Have you ever used this style yourself?

_____

_____

_____

_____

Analyzers We Have Known

Recently, at one of my one-day influence training programs, a woman approached me with a comment about her boss.

"I'm an extrovert and my boss is not," she said. "I go into his office with some urgent issues wanting to explore options and generate some new ideas. I do most of the talking, and when I'm finished I've already figured out what to do, and I do what I think is necessary. Well, about two days later he comes to me with *his* ideas on what to do. I'm stunned and tell him I've already taken care of it! I'm always amazed at how long it takes him to mull over and analyze the issues."

THE ANALYZER:

- prefers to deal with (and focus on) facts and information.
- makes decisions logically and carefully.
- is slow-paced.
- is reluctant to decide without having all the information.
- wants to be "in the know."

As meticulous as they can be frustrating, Analyzers rely heavily on logic, analysis, and command of the details. They decide logically and carefully, balancing and weighing all the facts and outlining the tradeoffs and options involved in the decision. They like to build on existing ideas and on structure with which they are already familiar. But they can be slow to act, always wanting more facts. They are often not comfortable in situations where there's no easy answer or clear-cut resolution.

Analyzers are likely to say things like:

- "I need a lot more time and information before I can get back to you."
- "Can you show me proof that this has worked before?"
- "I need a full report on this matter before I can act on it."
- "You/I/we need to do your/my/our homework."

The Analyzer and You

What is your reaction to the analyzer style of communication? Who do you know who uses this style?

_____

_____

_____

_____

Do you need to change your reaction to this style?

_____

_____

_____

_____

Have you ever used this style yourself?

_____

_____

_____

_____

Visionaries We Have Known

Jason had his work cut out for him. For his company's annual leadership conference, he was asked to make a presentation to some senior managers on a new product idea his team had developed. He desperately needed the managers to give the "thumbs up" to take the product to the next level of development.

From previous projects, Jason knew that two of these managers were real "analyzers," bottom line, data people. All he had to do was provide them with the facts they needed to build a good case for them.

But the third manager was an unknown to Jason, a new player. "What will it take for me to influence him?" Jason wondered.

But as he listened to this third manager speak about his marketing background, his "vision" for the company in the next few years, saying he could "imagine a new generation of product processes," Jason quickly identified him as having strong visionary preferences and tailored his presentation to him accordingly.

Sure enough, Jason got the "thumbs up" from the new manager. "You've really done your homework," the manager told him. "Not many project leaders think on the larger scale. I'm impressed."

THE VISIONARY:

- prefers to deal with "The Big Picture."
- makes decisions quickly, even impulsively.
- focuses on ideas rather than details.
- is fast-paced.
- wants to share the vision with others.
- wants to be in the spotlight.

Visionaries communicate in broad, general terms. They don't "sweat the small stuff." They tend to deal with "global issues," and look more to what *can be* rather than *what is*. Excited by ideas, newness, and novelty, they welcome change and enjoy exploring future possibilities. They make decisions quickly, sometimes too quickly, without considering the impact or repercussions of their decisions, or they base them on incomplete or insufficient facts.

Visionaries are likely to say things like:
- "Change is good."
- "As I see it, here's how we can make it happen."
- "Let's look at the big picture here."
- "Imagine this. . . ."
- "I want to be remembered for. . . ."

The Visionary and You

What is your reaction to the visionary style of communication? Who do you know who uses this style?

_____

_____

_____

_____

Do you need to change your reaction to this style?

_____

_____

_____

_____

Have you ever used this style yourself?

_____

_____

_____

_____

Supporters We Have Known

Karen knew there was something missing from the task force on change decisions she was putting together. She had representatives from all the major divisions across her organization, but felt uneasy that they were fast-trackers who often made decisions too quickly without considering the political implications, or how those decisions could derail a project in the future. She desperately needed a "people person," a common ground-seeker who could work with these hard-driving personalities.

Her former manager Sharon was such a person, a good listener, great at reaching consensus in difficult meetings, and skilled at balancing the make-up of team members. She was just the "supporter" type Karen needed, someone comfortable hearing all opinions and gaining commitment.

THE SUPPORTER:

- prefers to deal with (and focus on) people.
- makes decisions in the context of relationships.
- is more cautious before taking action.
- wants input from all involved parties.
- wants to be "in the loop."

Supporters are what we popularly call "people persons," good listeners and deeply empathic. They like to work on projects that have meaning to them, particularly those projects that benefit people over, or in addition to, the profit motive or their own power. They tend to look for common ground and points of agreement. They share their concerns and are usually willing to listen to yours. They are hesitant to make a decision until they have a clear understanding of the impact, particularly on the people involved in, or affected by, the decision. They may be uncomfortable making decisions that are not agreed to by all, or that may have unwelcome repercussions for some people. They may try to get wholehearted approval, even from people who may not be centrally involved in, or affected by, a decision.

Supporters are likely to say things like:

- "I'm sure there's another side to this issue."
- "I want everyone's voice to be heard before we make a decision on this."
- "I'm anxious about what this is going to mean for. . . ."
- "We have to try to reach a decision that's going to work for everyone."
- "Talk to me. What are your concerns? Let me figure out how I can help you."

The Supporter and You

What is your reaction to the supporter style of communication? Who do you know who uses this style?

_____

_____

_____

_____

Do you need to change your reaction to this style?

_____

_____

_____

_____

Have you ever used this style yourself?

_____

_____

_____

_____

When Styles Collide

Trouble can ensue when communication styles collide. Consider this story that one of my clients, a manufacturing engineer, told me after he'd learned the four communication styles:

"I report to at least three different managers on three different projects at any one time. When trying to influence these managers, I've always approached them with the same logic and data-driven arguments, but I always get mixed results. Now I realize that one of my managers is a 'big picture' person, what you call a Visionary, Alan.

"The other manager who really frustrates me is definitely more an Authoritarian in style. He wants the bottom-line first, details later, just the opposite of the way I'd naturally approach him.

"Now I realize I must approach each of them with behaviors they're comfortable with. I have to speak the language of their personal communication style if I'm going to influence them successfully. Thanks, Alan!"

 # Building Your Strategy

Keeping in mind that very few people operate with only one style, but usually with at least two (a primary style and a secondary style), determine which two styles are your own preference? Why? How do you think they work for you? Against you? Tackle these questions in Worksheet 19.

The Four Communication Styles

Which two styles do you prefer?

_____

_____

_____

Why? How do they work for you?

_____

_____

_____

How do they work against you?

_____

_____

_____

 ## A Minute of Your Time

Now, go back to the subject person in your personal influence situation. Based on your own experience with your subject, or on what you have been told by others who have dealt with this person, determine the two communication styles you believe to be their preference.

Later, we will use this information to help determine which combination of key behaviors would likely work best with your subject and to help determine pitfalls in dealing with them you would want to predict.

CHAPTER FIVE

Putting Together a Complete Influence Strategy

Effective influencing isn't just about having all the right influence tools. It's about knowing which ones to use, when, and in what order. That is what we will cover in this chapter. Not only will you learn the remaining two components to the complete formula for putting together a powerful influence edge strategy for any situation, you will also work through the complete strategy on a sample scenario provided in this section.

Before turning to the scenario, stop for a moment and consider the below planning sequence. These four steps represent the complete formula for devising an influence strategy. You are already familiar with the first two steps, and we will be covering the second two very soon:

1. Identifying Situational Factors
2. Identifying Behaviors

3. Determining the Behavior Sequence
4. Distancing Strategy

WORKING THE STRATEGY STEPS: THE LESLIE PROBLEM

Pretend you are a manager at a dynamic company. You support a group of field engineers who rely on you to understand their needs and to seek out training opportunities and other resources for them to carry out their jobs well and support the company's business units. Recently, Leslie, a quality control manager, has been initiating changes to established procedures that have left the field engineers confused and without a clear understanding of why her changes are necessary. The field engineers have sent you several voice mails and emails asking for clarification.

This has caught you by surprise because Leslie has basically left you out of the communication loop by not informing you of her changes before she announced them to your engineers. This isn't good because you *have* to be pre-informed of such changes before they are released so you can clarify points with her and be ready to explain and justify the new rules to your people when they come to you with angry, confused questions. But how to get Leslie, who isn't the most cooperative person in the world, to pull you into the communication loop? Clearly, you need a good influence strategy. Where do you begin?

Strategy Step One: Identifying Situational Factors

Culling what you can from this scenario (and using your own imagination when appropriate), refer back to the section on the two fundamental factors. What are the two fundamental factors of this situation? After you have written down your responses to this question, consider what is provided below.

Your responses should look something like this:

What is your goal and what do you want?

Have Leslie get my approval when she sends memos to field managers relating to my area. Establish a better working relationship with Leslie.

Who do you need to influence?

Leslie.

By when?

Immediately.

How will you know if you get what you want?

Leslie will run her memos by me before she sends them out to my engineers. No more of her directives going out without my knowing.

What assumptions are you making?

She's trying to take over. Wants to look good. Doesn't care about me. Likes the "big picture." Lacks detail in her planning.

How might the other person think of you in relation to the situation?

Controlling, authoritarian.

What does this person think of the situation?

She thinks it's poor.

What can you do to make it easier for the other person to agree?

Show some flexibility about all communications that go out. There may be some I don't need to see.

What are the goals of the other person's organization?

Leslie's department needs to increase service to field offices.

What is currently happening in the other person's organization?

Leslie's department has had two people resign.

Strategy Step Two: Identifying Behaviors

Now it's time to pinpoint which combination of the key behaviors you should use in your meeting with Leslie. Using the checklist below, determine which situations and behaviors correspond with the Leslie scenario. Circle the corresponding behaviors. Remember, you want to choose enough behaviors so that they

PUSH SITUATIONS	BEHAVIOR
You believe the other person does not have a high need to control and may be uncertain or uncommitted on how to proceed.	Assert
You and the other person are relatively unemotional about the situation. The person is probably open to hearing your suggestions.	Suggest
PULL SITUATIONS	**BEHAVIOR**
You want additional information and are interested in what the other person has to say. You want the other person to be involved and feel a sense of commitment. You are open to alternatives.	Ask (open-ended) Questions and
You think the other person may be hesitant about the goal but needs to take responsibility for resolving the issue. You want the other person to identify alternatives.	Ask (focused) Questions
It is important that you show the other person that you understand her position or point of view. The other person may be upset or emotional. You think there may be some underlying issues that the other person has not confronted.	Summarize
PUSH/PULL SITUATIONS	**BEHAVIOR**
You have control over incentives and are willing to give them. You believe that getting the other person fully committed to your idea is not as important as getting the person to comply.	Offer Incentives

follow through to a resolution (and don't forget your "back-up" behavior), but not so many that you will have a hard time sequencing them in the next strategy step. (Three choices is probably fine.)

Strategy Step Three: Determining the Behavior Sequence

Now that you have circled the behaviors you think will be most effective in the situation with Leslie, you have to decide the best order in which to use them, how you are going to play your cards, so to speak. Here is one area of the influence edge where there is really no formula, but where you can rely on your own intuitiveness, and your own understanding of the specific goal you are seeking.

Put the behaviors in order for the situation with Leslie. As you do, you might want to think about what your opening words would be to activate each behavior, and your rationale for trying each one, and for placing them in the order you have chosen. This should help you create a loose, flexible "script" for your upcoming influence encounter.

For example, let's say the behaviors you circled as you went down the list were: Suggest, Ask (open-ended) Questions, Summarize, and Offer Incentives. Your sequence, along with opening words and rationale, might look like this:
1. Suggest.
Wording: "I'd like to make a suggestion that from now on, you email me a draft of your new change policy announcements so I can skim it, go over any questions with you, and pre-inform my engineers so they don't come to me with confusion and questions later on."

Rationale: You want to give Leslie a "soft" suggestion giving some direction but not pushing her too hard.

2. Ask (open-ended) Questions.
Opening words: "How can we go about making this work for

<table>
<tr><td>

**An Offer
She Couldn't Refuse**

Finding a mentor is never easy, but being aware of how someone you want to be your mentor would like to be approached is a key to initiating a successful, long-lasting relationship.

At a recent conference for women in business, a very high-level executive told me this: "I'm always an influence subject for bright young women in my industry who are seeking a mentor. Unfortunately, my time and resources are limited, and I have to turn most of these prospective mentees away.

"But recently, one sharp young financial analyst impressed me differently. Instead of asking for my mentorship and giving reasons why we would make a good match, she offered to help me research and develop new business software for my division. It had been reported in the company newsletter recently that this was something I was interested in, and she'd obviously done her homework. And she came to me not just wanting something, but offering something too. I thought, now here's someone I can invest time in.

"A year later, we're still in a mentor-mentee relationship."

</td></tr>
</table>

us? What would be the easiest way of doing this for you?"

Rationale: You want to let Leslie know you are open to alternatives or alterations in your suggestion, giving her a chance to be part of the process.

3. Summarize.

Opening words: "So what you suggest we do is . . . ; so what you want is . . . ; so what you're saying is . . . ."

Rationale: After Leslie responds to your suggestion, you want to make sure you are both "on the same page," that you heard her correctly. If you didn't, you want her to have the chance to clarify herself.

4. Offer Incentive(s).

Opening words: "I'd be willing to . . . (run my own memos to employees in the quality control department by you first so they didn't create any surprise visits to your office), if you'd be willing to . . . (do the same for me).

Rationale: If Leslie resists your suggestion, you want to try to close the deal and create a win–win feeling.

Strategy Step Four: Distancing Strategy

Now, keep in mind that even though there are four behaviors sequenced here, you may not need to work through all of them. For example, if you happen to catch Leslie the day her new mahogany credenza is delivered, she may be in such a good mood that, as soon as you broach your suggestion, she says, "Sure, that sounds fine, don't worry about it." (If this is the case, you might want to repeat your suggestion back to her in explicit detail to be sure she agrees.) And if she makes alterations to your suggestion which become apparent when you repeat them back to her, then you don't need to move to the fourth behavior option, which is to engage her interest with an incentive. Everybody is happy.

But what if you run through your program of chosen behaviors, and you have gotten nowhere—or even exacerbated the situation?

What if, for example, Leslie adamantly resists your suggestion that she run her changes by you first via email? In such instances it's often helpful to keep asking open-ended questions and summarizing the other person's answers until you have helped articulate the person's true wants. For example:

Leslie: "No, emailing you a draft won't work for me at all."

You: "Can you give me some sense of why that wouldn't work?"

Leslie: "Because you know the boss wants me to post change announcements as soon as we decide on them. You're hardly ever at your desk, and I'd probably have to wait at least overnight for you to read my emails and for us to go over them."

You: "Can you suggest a way we could go through that process faster?"

Leslie: "Honestly, if I called you or left you a voice message saying I had the new announcements, you'd have to go over them immediately so I wouldn't lose time getting them out."

You: "Well, I do check my voice messages several times a day, often from somebody else's phone. If, when I got your messages, I made them high priority and came straight to your office as soon as possible to go over them with you, would that work?"

Leslie: (sighing wearily) "Yes, I suppose I could do that."

You: "So what you want me to do is come look over your announcements with you as soon as you inform me that they've been drafted, right?"

Leslie: "Right. I'm pretty sure that might work."

But what if even this tactic of continued question-asking and summarizing fails? What if, in response to your suggestion that she think of a way you could accelerate the review process, Leslie responds:

"You know, I have a dozen people waiting for me over in systems development right now. I just don't have the time to sit here and figure out how to accommodate you."

Clearly, this is a good time to distance yourself from Leslie and the situation. You might respond:

"Okay, I understand that. Could you just look at your calendar briefly and tell me a good time for you in the next few days for us to sit down again and figure out how to do this review process in the way that's easiest and fastest for you?"

But what if Leslie's response is:

"There is no easy or fast way to do it, because knowing you and your hairsplitting work style, we'll be haggling over the changes for two weeks before you're happy with them."

Again, *distancing* is clearly called for in such an instance where the situation seems to be becoming too hot to handle. You might respond (after taking a deep breath, of course):

- "Okay, I'm not sure we're getting what we need out of this meeting. Why don't we take a ten-minute break and think about where we're at, then come back to it?"
- "Okay, why don't we both put all our thoughts about the issue in a memo to each other, and once we've both read them, we'll meet again in person to figure this out?"
- "Okay, I was hoping we could resolve this ourselves, but maybe we should invite Ben (a respected colleague, etc.) to sit in with us. He could be a neutral third party who can help us facilitate the meeting."

Remember, what you want to do is protect the relationship temporarily so you can revisit it and influence. Even though you may seem to have hit a wall with Leslie, distancing yourself from her and the issue is an important part of *managing* the influence process in a crisis.

CHAPTER SIX

Practice Scenarios for Increasing Your Influence Skills

In this chapter, we are going to take everything you have learned thus far and apply it to the personal influence situation that you first outlined in Worksheet 4, and that you have been revisiting frequently throughout the workbook. By the time you have completed the work in this section, you should be ready to approach your influence subject with the first strategy steps toward getting what you want or need from this person.

STRATEGY STEP ONE: IDENTIFYING SITUATIONAL FACTORS

Okay, go back to your personal influence situation and think through responses for the following questions addressing the two fundamental factors. Remember, if you have to enact an influence strategy with someone on the spot and you only have time for one strategy step, *this is the one to do.*

Your Goal

- What do you want? _____

  _____

  _____

- Whom do you need to influence? _____

  _____

- By when? _____

  _____

- How will you know if you achieve your goal? _____

  _____

  _____

- What assumptions are you making about the other person?

  _____

  _____

  About the overall situation? _____

  _____

  _____

The Other Person

- How might the other person think of you in relation to the situation? _____

  _____

  _____

- What can you do to make it easier for the other person to agree? _____

_____

- What are the goals of the other person's organization? If you and your subject are in the same organization, ask yourself What are the goals of the other person's department/ division/team/etc.?_____

_____

_____

_____

STRATEGY STEP TWO: IDENTIFYING BEHAVIORS

Just like you did for the situation with Leslie, read the list below and determine which situations and behaviors correspond with your personal influence situation. Circle the corresponding behaviors. Remember, you want to choose behaviors so that they get you close to a resolution (and don't forget your "back-up" behavior), but not so many that you will have a hard time sequencing them in the next strategy step. (Three is probably enough, but of course, it's *your* situation and thus *your* choice.)

PUSH SITUATIONS	BEHAVIOR
You believe the other person does not have a high need to control and may be uncertain or uncommitted on how to proceed.	Assert
You and the other person are relatively unemotional about the situation. The person is probably open to hearing your suggestions.	Suggest

PULL SITUATIONS	BEHAVIOR
You want additional information and are interested in what the other person has to say. You want the other person to be involved and feel a sense of commitment. You are open to alternatives.	Ask (open-ended) Questions
	and
You think the other person may be hesitant about the goal but needs to take responsibility for resolving the issue. You want the other person to identify alternatives.	Ask (focused) Questions
It is important that you show the other person that you understand her position or point of view. The other person may be upset or emotional. You think there may be some underlying issues that the other person has not confronted.	Summarize

PUSH/PULL SITUATIONS	BEHAVIOR
You have control over incentives and are willing to give them. You believe that getting the other person fully committed to your idea is not as important as getting the person to comply.	Offer Incentives

STRATEGY STEP THREE: DETERMINING THE BEHAVIOR SEQUENCE

Now it's time to take the behaviors you circled and figure out the order in which you want to use them. As you sequence your behaviors (see below), think through possible wordings for the moment when you use them with your subject, as well as your rationale for putting each one where you did in the sequence. Remember, you can always refer back to this step in the Leslie situation from the previous section.

BEHAVIOR	POSSIBLE WORDING	RATIONALE
1.		
2.		
3.		
4.		

STRATEGY STEP FOUR: DISTANCING STRATEGY

Now that you have chosen, sequenced, and even worded your behaviors, ask yourself these two questions:

1. At what point would I abandon my chosen behaviors and seek to temporarily distance myself from my subject and the situation? What kind of response from the subject would compel me to distance myself?

_____

_____

_____

_____

2. How would I do so? What would the wording be? Here are some helpful hints concerning the second questions. You might:
   • change the subject, if the issue gets too hot.

- suggest taking a short break, time to think or cool off.
- suggest that you and your subject postpone discussing the situation to a later date, so that either or both of you can gather more data, consult with other people, etc.

_____

_____

_____

_____

_____

_____

_____

Let's Put Some Space Between Us

I was in a meeting with three clients from a major insurance company, helping them design a new management curriculum. Things seemed to be going fine when, as we started talking about the use of a 360-degree feedback instrument, one of the key stakeholders jumped up forcefully. "My people *do not like* 360-degree feedback, and they *won't* use it!"

We all just sat there, stunned. This issue had obviously hit a nerve with this important individual, and the outburst seemed totally out-of-character with her otherwise open communication style. But I didn't want the meeting to break apart or diverge from the positive track we'd been on. How was I to disengage temporarily from this one sticky issue without calling off the whole meeting?

Thankfully, one of the other managers knew just what to do (which proves that trainers can learn from clients as much as the other way around). "It's always difficult to decide on the best way to get our managers feedback, so why don't we table the discussion of the 360-degree approach until we do more research on it and determine possible options?"

A collective sigh of relief could be heard in the room, including the manager who'd gotten so upset. Later, I found out she'd had a bad experience with 360-degree feedback at another company, where it had been misused.

WHEN TO USE THE KEY BEHAVIORS: A CLOSER LOOK

You have just taken your first crack at walking your own personal influence situation through the influence edge strategy—congratulations! Maybe you found that choosing the right behaviors, laying them out in the right order, wording them, and even determining a back-up or "distancing" plan all fell easily into place. At the very least, you should have a better, more systematic, understanding of your influence situation (from your point of view and your subject's point of view) and what you need to do to turn it into a win/win situation.

However, if you are still unsure about matching your behaviors to the specific quirks or nuances of your influence situation (and no two are alike), or even if you would just like more practice, then you might benefit from the following guide, which offers a somewhat more in-depth picture of what behaviors to use in what situations. The guide also includes some key questions you might want to ask yourself before you use these behaviors. (As a general rule, if, for each behavior, you answer "yes" to more than one of the questions, it's highly likely that that behavior will work well in your situation.)

BEHAVIOR	USE WHEN	QUESTIONS TO CONSIDER
Push Behavior: Assert This is an often-misunderstood behavior. People sometimes confuse assertion with aggression. However, if used properly, assertion will get you closer to what you want than almost any other behavior. Asserting is letting the other party know exactly what you want. Having the skill to ask for something directly can help you get more in business and life in general. There are people out there you may want to influence who will not listen to anything unless it is framed in assertive language.	• Use when being direct is needed. • Use when you want to be seen as in charge.	• From an outsider's perspective, would your needs be considered reasonable? • Do you believe that the other person does not have a high need to control this or any situation? • Do you get a sense that the other person does not have a clear idea of what needs to be done or how to proceed?
Push Behavior: Suggest It's important to keep in mind that when you make a suggestion, the other person might well ask, "why should I act on that?" Therefore, always be ready to communicate the reasons and benefits behind the suggestion in order to cultivate the interest of the other person.	• Use when the other person appears open for a suggestion. • Use when a softer, more reasonable approach is needed.	• Would others consider you to be objective in this situation and willing to look at both sides rationally? • Do you believe that you and the other person are relatively unemotional about the situation? • Do you get any signals from the other person that he wants suggestions on how to proceed?
Pull Behavior: Ask Questions (both open-ended and focused) It's important to remember the difference between these two kinds of questions. Open-ended questions are asked to gather information and to find out what the other person is thinking, while focused questions help the other person focus on specific, concrete alternatives.	• Ask open-ended questions when you are seeking as much information as possible. • Ask open-ended questions when you want to be seen as open to alternatives. • Ask focused questions when you want the other person to identify possible incentives. • Ask focused questions when you are seeking a way to "close" the deal.	• Do you want to get information, and are you interested in what the other person has to say? • Do you believe that getting the other person's commitment is important to the accomplishment of the goal? • After hearing what the other person has to say, would you be willing to modify your original goal, or is your goal rigidly established? • Do you think the other person will be hesitant about the goal, but will still feel the need to take responsibility for resolving the issue? • Are you willing to go with potential solutions that the other person might offer? • Do you think the other person has not considered various alternatives and that it would be important to do so?

BEHAVIOR	USE WHEN	QUESTIONS TO CONSIDER
Pull Behavior: Summarize Summarizing what someone has said to you is a good way to clarify issues that have come up in an influence situation. Summarization is also a good way to demonstrate understanding.	• Use when the other person needs evidence that you've listened. • Use when the other person is upset or angry. • Use when there are multiple, complex issues at play. • Use when you want to appear even-handed in your consideration.	• Do you think it will be important to show the other person that you understand her point of view? • Do you think the issue is complex, and that you will need to make sure you and the other person understand key points along the way? • Do you think the other person may be upset or emotional and will need your help in calming down? • Do you believe the other person trusts you and your motives? • Do you think the other person will be unsure or confused about how to proceed? • Do you believe there may be some underlying issues in the situation that the person has not confronted?
Push/Pull Behavior: Offer Incentives Something all influencers must assume is that people want something from them. Whether the other person is a boss, peer, customer, or member of another team, she will be thinking "what's in it for me?" or "what's in it for my team?" To offer an incentive can be very powerful. An incentive is an item of exchange, something that the other person sees as value. The incentive may be tangible or intangible, and it should be something that appeals to or benefits the other party.	• Use when the other person may need to know specifically how he or she will benefit. • Use when you need an agreement to resolve a conflict.	• Have you thought of something that you can provide to the other person to make it easier for him to agree with you? If you offer, are you truly willing to give it? • Do you think it's okay to get the other person to agree to do what you want him to do without the other person's being fully committed to the goal? • Would the other person see you as trying to be fair in your exchange?

MORE PRACTICE SCENARIOS FOR MASTERING THE KEY BEHAVIORS

Just as a really good set of toolbox instructions provides you with as many vivid, real-life applications as possible, the following scenarios are meant to give you even more practice determining what behaviors you might use and how you might use them in a variety of situations. The scenarios presented here are fairly broad. Hopefully, you will be able to apply the basic formulae to more specific influence situations that have occurred in your own life.

Practice Scenario One

The marketing team you lead at a major software development company needs to fully understand the technology of a new computer-aided design program developed by the brilliant-but-uncommunicative Wanda Johnson, a content expert on another team. You want to influence Wanda to teach your team the various ways potential customers can use this new program, but, as usual, she seems reluctant to give your team the time it needs to familiarize itself successfully with the program. You also sense that training your team is a low priority with Wanda, who always wants to return to creating new programs once a developmental cycle has concluded. You have arranged a short meeting with her, and you know this may be your only opportunity to influence.

What would you do? Take a stab at it in Worksheet 20, then compare your ideas against those I have provided after the worksheet.

Practice Makes It Perfect

SCENARIO ONE

1. What would you do? How would you approach this situation?

_____

_____

_____

_____

2. What would be your bottom line goal?

_____

_____

_____

_____

3. Behaviors you might use?

_____

_____

_____

_____

Below are some possible strategies for how to influence Wanda:

1. Suggest: "I'd like to suggest that we look at a couple of ways to get my team up to speed faster. This would really help us and the customer at the same time."

2. Summarize: "So you're saying that your time is completely filled right now, but you'd be glad to give my group a complete overview in two weeks?"

3. Ask (focused) Questions: "Could we format the training more flexibly so we might move that time up to a week to 10 days instead?"

Practice Scenario Two

You have just heard that Kay Brown, your manager at StarTech, an internet service provider, is just about ready to assign a new project to Weston Sanchez, one of your peers. About a week ago you dropped a really big hint to Kay that you wanted the project. You don't know what the exact situation is, but you do know that this project represents an opportunity to demonstrate your skills, and you want the assignment as project leader. Now you and Kay are about to have a meeting.

What would you do? Take a stab at it in Worksheet 21, then compare your ideas against those I have provided after the worksheet.

Practice Makes It Perfect

SCENARIO TWO

1. What would you do? How would you approach this situation?

_____

_____

_____

_____

2. What would be your bottom line goal?

_____

_____

_____

_____

3. Behaviors you might use?

_____

_____

_____

_____

Below are some possible strategies for how to influence Kay:

1. Ask (open-ended) Questions: "Kay, what's the status of the FiveStar project? How do you see it developing?"

2. Ask (focused) Questions: "What would make you feel comfortable assigning the FiveStar Project to me?"

3. Summarize: "Are you saying that my skills don't fit this specific role, and that maybe at this time I'd be biting off more than I could chew with FiveStar?"

4. Offer Incentives: "If I were to show you that I've used similar skills before and have the time right now to handle this project, would you consider assigning it to me?"

Practice Scenario Three

You have just come home from a board meeting at Fairlawn Country Club, where a fellow board member, George W. Smith, questioned your loyalty to "the Fairlawn family." You were unable to say anything at the meeting and now you want to meet for a round of golf with Smith to clear the air and make sure he doesn't say things like that about you again.

What would you do? Take a stab at it in Worksheet 22, then compare your ideas against those I have provided after the worksheet.

Practice Makes It Perfect

SCENARIO THREE

1. What would you do? How would you approach this situation?

_____

_____

_____

_____

2. What would be your bottom line goal?

_____

_____

_____

_____

3. Behaviors you might use?

_____

_____

_____

_____

Below are some possible strategies for how to influence George:

1. Assert: "I'd like to spend some time with you, George. We can play a round of golf and talk about what happened at the board meeting today."

2. Summarize (to check understanding): "My understanding is that you made comments at the meeting about my inability to resolve the chlorination problem, and I'm concerned that it appears like I haven't been doing my job well."

3. Ask (open-ended) Questions: "Is this how you see the issues?"

4. Ask (focused) Questions: "How can we avoid this kind of misunderstanding in the future?" Or, "What can I do to show you I have done my job successfully?"

Practice Scenario Four

You are about to meet with Paige Turner, your fellow editorial director at the romance publishing house, who has talked to you about a problem with deciding how steamy jacket covers should be. You both agree that there is a problem, but disagree on the way to solve it. Now you have additional information you want to present to get Paige to agree with you on how to proceed.

What would you do? Take a stab at it in Worksheet 23, then compare your ideas against those I have provided after the worksheet.

Practice Makes It Perfect

SCENARIO FOUR

1. What would you do? How would you approach this situation?

_____

_____

_____

_____

2. What would be your bottom line goal?

_____

_____

_____

_____

3. Behaviors you might use?

_____

_____

_____

_____

Below are some possible strategies for how to influence Paige:

1. Summarize: "In our last discussion, you outlined a problem with the jacket covers, and brought up an alternative to my suggested course of action."

2. Ask (focused) Questions: "What would it take to have one of your editors work with one of mine to get this jacket thing resolved?"

 ## A Minute of Your Time

Now that you've had a chance to work through the four practice scenarios, take a minute to reflect on what you've learned. Remember that these scenarios are fairly broad in detail and impact. Your real-life influence situation will be more narrow in scope, of course, full of the specific challenges that make it unique. The last chapter of this workbook is designed to help you move from broad scenarios to more narrow real-life challenges by giving you some tips on how to hone your influence skills.

CHAPTER SEVEN

Honing Your Influence Edge by Building Rapport

Now that you know how to put the influence edge strategy into practice, you may be wondering, what more is there to know? Well, believe it or not, there is one more incredibly important element we have yet to talk about. This element is *rapport*—that seemingly magical dynamic between two people, that "click" that makes it a joy and a pleasure to interact with another person as colleague, friend, lover . . . or sometimes, as a combination of all three! And of course, rapport is vastly helpful in an influence situation.

I call rapport seemingly magical because, like the powers of influence themselves, it's not necessarily something that is there naturally from the beginning or naturally not there. Sure, sometimes rapport between two people is destined to happen, but that doesn't mean that, if you want a better working

Whoever Said Rapport Wasn't Built in a Day?

Consultants in my business are always telling their audiences and clients that most work gets done through good working relationships. Yet always the following question remains: how do you establish these relationships, when clearly the skills for this kind of approach to business requires time and energy, two ingredients that are in short supply in today's fast-moving companies?

My answer is basically this: building a relationship can be done easily, in five minutes of strategically placed conversation. It doesn't take five hours! One of my clients, an engineer at a high-tech firm, asked me for a quick fix to a rough peer relationship he had to improve. I asked him if he could give it five minutes a day of concentrated influence.

He said, "Sure, I guess it's worth five minutes a day if I could turn this relationship around."

I told him simply to seek common ground with this person—that he shouldn't Push this person at all during these five minutes but should focus on what they had in common and express this commonality directly. I told him that the best influencers can find commonalties between themselves and most anyone.

That was a real challenge for this engineer, a very assertive person. Two weeks later, though, he emailed me to say that although he and his peer still didn't agree on most issues, their relationship had markedly improved, and he could see now that he and his influence subject had much in common.

This was their first step to a "good working relationship."

relationship with someone, you can't build rapport—which, at its basis, is simply the ability to sustain good communication with the other person, even when you strongly disagree on an issue. If you want good rapport in a relationship where it's not already there, however, the process has to start with you.

So how do you "build" rapport? Well, gearing your approach to your subject's preferred communication style (Authoritarian, Analyzer, Visionary, or Supporter) is one way to go about it. Another is to familiarize yourself with the way your subject's mind works. How we perceive the world, process information, and communicate corresponds to three principal senses:

1. Vision
2. Hearing
3. Feeling

These three senses (smell and taste are used to a lesser extent) make up what are called our representational systems, and we communicate by speaking the language of one, two, or all three. When we can speak to another person in the language of their preferred representational system, we build greater understanding, strengthen our rapport with them, and increase our ability to influence. We are "talking their talk," or "speaking their language" as it were. There's no special trick to this. It just requires that we listen to the other person carefully enough so that we can identify their preferred approach to communication. That way we can best determine not only effective influence behaviors, but also how to deliver our message.

Because each representational system has its own language, you can tell a person's predominant approach to communication by the words she uses. When you respond to the words by using similar language, the other person has a sense that she is being heard correctly . . . and rapport is further established.

THE THREE REPRESENTATIONAL SYSTEMS

Visual People:

- think by creating pictures or writing notes.
- select pictures from memory to make sense out of things.
- tend to use primarily visual words like "look," "see," and "picture."
- can easily recall colors and shapes.
- are often affected by the color of the room, and the order (or disorder) of things around them.

Visual Words and Phrases

Envision	View
Clear	Graphic
Hidden	Notice
Appears to me	Get a perspective on
In light of	Looks like
Makes a scene	Mental image
Mind's eye	Paint a picture
Plainly see	See to it
Up front	Well-defined
Short-sighted	In view of

Influence Examples Using Visual Language

Assert: "I need a clear plan from you that shows me each feature's release schedule and development costs."

Suggest: "It looks like we should adjourn the meeting

Getting Through to a Visual Type

Jan, a client of mine, needed to sell her boss, the vice president of information services, her idea on a new software package.

"Contrary to what everyone believes about IT people, my boss definitely doesn't like dwelling on the details of an idea," she confided to me one sunny afternoon on the patio of her company's cafeteria. "He never read the proposals I used to spend days putting together for him. He's a purely visual person. He wants to see pictures. I've got to give him the whole picture at once, details come later, if at all.

"My new approach is to supply him with colorful graphics that create a summary of my case and give him a clear mental image."

Jan is currently training other staff members how to approach the vice president successfully. "They've got to learn to be strategic," she said, "to think in different modes, if they're going to survive here."

An Auditory Type Speaks Out

"The first thing I do with new members of my team," a manager at a high-tech company once told me, "is instruct them how to successfully influence me. I hired these people because they're the best and brightest, and they can add real value to our efforts. I don't want them frustrated and upset because they can't hold my attention or sell me on their ideas.

" 'Be prepared to talk to me,' I tell them. 'Give me the details so that we can discuss them.' I want to hear their ideas clearly so we can kick them around, listen to all sides of the issues and make the right decisions."

now, follow-up on our action items, and regroup when we can draw conclusions based on a complete picture."

Ask (open-ended) Questions: "How does this look to you?"

Auditory People:

- think by creating an internal dialogue.
- consider it important to speak well.
- tend to use primarily auditory words such as "call," "discuss," and "sounds good."
- can easily recall what someone said to them.
- become disoriented with too much environmental noise.

Auditory Words and Phrases

Petition	Ringing
Resonant	Told
Loud	Silent
Shout	Talk
Request	Ask
Afterthought	Clearly expressed
Call on	Describe in detail
Earful	Express yourself
Give an account of	Give me your ears
Grant an audience	Hidden message
Voice an opinion	Well-informed
Within hearing range	Word for word

Influence Examples Using Auditory Language

Suggest: "I suggest that I describe in detail why it is so important for you to address these issues."

Summarize: "Sounds to me that we both agree to discuss further before making a requested change to the system. We will orchestrate a process for handling change requests."

Offer Incentives: "If you will first listen to our proposal before you approach other vendors, I will address each of your concerns personally."

Kinesthetic People:

- think by getting in touch with feelings.
- tend to move around a great deal.
- tend to use kinesthetic words such as "touch," "feel," and "contact."
- rarely forget how they felt or were made to feel.
- tend to express emotions spontaneously when in public.

Kinesthetic Words and Phrases

Feel	Pressure
Hurt	Get the point
Graceful	Sensual
Irritated	Problem
Cool, calm, collected	Firm foundation
Floating on thin air	Get a handle on
Get a load of this	Get in touch with
Get the drift	Hand-in-hand
Know-how	Lay cards on table
Light-headed	Moment of panic
Stuffed shirt	Too much hassle
Topsy-turvy	Underhanded

Influence Examples Using Kinesthetic Language

Assert: "To get to the point, it's vital that I have close contact with the developers from the start."

Ask (focused) Questions: "What will it take to get you to pull some strings so we can meet the agreed-upon deadline?"

Spoken Like a True Kinesthetic Type

At a recent sales conference I attended, a national accounts director made the following remarks in his keynote address:

"These are high-pressure times we are selling in. We must focus on our goals like a laser beam. More than ever, the customer needs to be touched by you. Every call you make to a key customer is a moment of truth . . . an opportunity to lay a firm foundation."

As I watched the audience members nod their heads in agreement, it occurred to me that this speaker had really done his homework. He really knew his audience and was influencing them in their language, tapping into their emotions, and motivating them to go for more.

Building Your Strategy

Now let's try to identify which of the three is your own preferred type and approach. Relax, close your eyes, and picture yourself at 16 coming home from school and walking in the door of your house. What comes to mind first? Do you remember:

What you saw upon walking in?

What you heard?

Or do you first recall a particular feeling, say, a sense of relief at finally being within a safe haven after the stress and noise of the bus ride home? Or a tightening of the stomach, or quickening of your heartbeat, over some remembered tension and anxiety?

Whatever you recalled first—sights, sounds, or feelings—can give you valuable insight into which of the three representational systems you gravitate toward most easily. (Of course, this is not to say that you, or anyone else, don't use two of the systems, or even all three, variously, or at the same time—just that most of us do have a predominant mode we use most frequently.)

Now take a moment to think about the subject of your personal influence situation. Based on past conversations with this person, try to determine which of the three modes best reflects the way he thinks and speaks. Can you think of any words or "pet phrases" that are used again and again? Which of the three modes does the subject seem to fall under? How might you "mirror" some of the subject's preferred language in the wording of your behavior strategies? Take a stab at answering these questions in Worksheet 24.

Representational Systems and Your Influence Subject

In your situation, which of these three modes best reflects the way your subject thinks and speaks?

_____

_____

_____

How might you use these modes to "mirror" some of the preferred language in the wording of your behavior strategies?

_____

_____

_____

_____

_____

_____

Wrap-Up

Congratulations. You have walked through *all* the steps behind launching a powerful yet flexible influence edge strategy with your personal influence subject . . . and believe me, though the subject you used in the workbook may be the first person you influence with influence edge savvy, she certainly won't be the last! That's the great thing about this system—it's designed to be used again and again to transform the often disorderly and impossible-seeming task of getting someone else to help you achieve your goal into an entirely viable process of analysis, preparation, and action. In a new world where the opportunity to exert direct authority is rapidly declining (on and *off* the job), the influence edge strategy systematizes the "people skills" and persuasive powers necessary to get what you want or need from those most able to give it to you.

If you don't get the exact results you are seeking from your first experience using the skills outlined in this workbook, don't get discouraged. Again, a big part of making the influence edge work for you is building rapport with your subject, and that doesn't happen overnight. Feel free to work the strategy at your own pace (if your goal isn't on a deadline), adjusting its steps to your own needs, strengths, and weaknesses. I didn't write *The Influence Edge* to provide a quick-fix shortcut to getting what you want, but to empower you with interpersonal skills that will serve you well over a lifetime.

So before you embark on a real-life application of *The Influence Edge* to the personal influence situation you have worked on here, be sure to ask yourself what information you still need to make sure you approach your subject with the behaviors and language that will best help you influence. If you feel you need to gather more information to flesh out your analysis, then by all means do so. There's no such thing as being *too* prepared.

And remember . . . this workbook covered only the highlights of The Influence Edge workshop materials. If you are interested in learning the entire, power-packed program yourself, or if you want it for a team or your whole organization, don't hesitate to contact me at:

Vengel Consulting Group, Inc.
1230 Dutch Mill Drive
Danville, CA 94526
Tel: (925) 837-0148
email: alan@vengelconsulting.com

About the Author

With over twenty years experience as a consultant, speaker, and educator in management training and organizational development, Alan Vengel *knows* influence. A founder of Vengel Consulting Group, Inc. and a strategic partner with Beverly Kaye and Associates, Inc./Career Systems International, he has conducted over 2,000 seminars in management and leadership development. He has also developed and is a master trainer for the acclaimed skill-building programs The Negotiation Focus™, The EMail Edge™, and The Influence Edge™, which is presented here.

He has developed, presented, and installed programs in performance management, leadership development, and career development strategies in hundreds of organizations. His recent clients include Nortel Networks, Cisco Systems, Fireman's Fund, Intel, KLA, Quantum, Compaq Computers, The Gas Company, Xerox, and LSI Logic.

Vengel is a frequent speaker for both industry and academia throughout the United States, Canada, Europe, and Asia. He has been an instructor in the College of Continuing Education at McGill University in Montreal, Canada, The University of Southern California in Los Angeles, and the University of California at Los Angeles, San Diego, and Santa Barbara. He has also served on the staff of the National Training Laboratories (NTL).

Vengel has an undergraduate degree from the University of Florida and an M.A. from the University of Arizona. He has studied organizational theory and management development at UCLA and has extensive experience in a great variety of industrial, business, educational, and government institutions.

Berrett-Koehler Publishers

BERRETT-KOEHLER is an independent publisher of books, periodicals, and other publications at the leading edge of new thinking and innovative practice on work, business, management, leadership, stewardship, career development, human resources, entrepreneurship, and global sustainability.

Since the company's founding in 1992, we have been committed to supporting the movement toward a more enlightened world of work by publishing books, periodicals, and other publications that help us to integrate our values with our work and work lives, and to create more humane and effective organizations.

We have chosen to focus on the areas of work, business, and organizations, because these are central elements in many people's lives today. Furthermore, the work world is going through tumultuous changes, from the decline of job security to the rise of new structures for organizing people and work. We believe that change is needed at all levels—individual, organizational, community, and global—and our publications address each of these levels.

We seek to create new lenses for understanding organizations, to legitimize topics that people care deeply about but that current business orthodoxy censors or considers secondary to bottom-line concerns, and to uncover new meaning, means, and ends for our work and work lives.

See next page for other books from Berrett-Koehler Publishers

Berrett-Koehler books and audios are available at quantity discounts for orders of 10 or more copies.

The Influence Edge

How to Persuade Others to Help You Achieve Your Goals

Alan A. Vengel

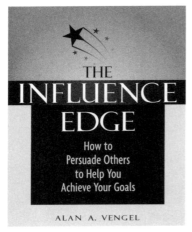

Paperback, 120 pages
ISBN 1-58376-156-X
Item #6156X-344 $15.95

To find out about discounts on orders of 10 or more copies for individuals, corporations, institutions and organizations, please call us toll-free at (800)929-2929.

To find out about our discount programs for resellers, please contact our Special Sales department at (415)288-0260; Fax: (415)362-2512. Or email us at bkpub@bkpub.com.

Berrett-Koehler Publishers
PO Box 565, Williston, VT 05495-9900
Call toll-free! **800-929-2929** 7 am-12 midnight
Or fax your order to 802-864-7627
For fastest service order online:
www.bkconnection.com

PeopleSmart
Developing Your Interpersonal Intelligence

Mel Silberman, Ph.D., with Freda Hansburg, Ph.D.

Everyone is in the people business, because all of us deal with other people all the time. That's why it's smart to reap the benefits of this eminently practical guide. *PeopleSmart* details the eight essential skills of interpersonal intelligence and provides a powerful plan for becoming more effective in every relationship—with supervisors, coworkers, a spouse, family, and friends.

Paperback original, 300 pages • ISBN 1-57675-091-4
Item #50914-344 $16.95

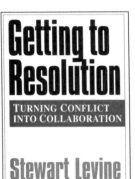

Getting to Resolution
Turning Conflict Into Collaboration

Stewart Levine

Stewart Levine gives readers an exciting new set of tools for resolving personal and business conflicts. Marriages run amuck, neighbors at odds with one another, business deals gone sour, and the pain and anger caused by corporate downsizing and layoffs are just a few of the conflicts he addresses.

Paperback, 240 pages • ISBN 1-57675-115-5
Item #51155-344 $16.95

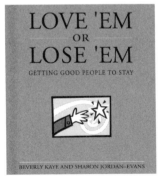

Love 'Em or Lose 'Em
Getting Good People to Stay

Beverly Kaye and Sharon Jordan-Evans

It happens time and time again: the brightest and most talented people leave the company for "better opportunities." Bigger salaries, loftier titles, and added perks may work for a while, but what employees really want are meaningful work, opportunities for growth, and excellent bosses. Beverly Kaye and Sharon Jordan-Evans explore the truth behind the dissatisfactions of today's workers and offer 26 strategies that managers can use keep them on the team.

Paperback original, 244 pages • ISBN 1-57675-073-6
Item #50736-344 $17.95

Berrett-Koehler Publishers
PO Box 565, Williston, VT 05495-9900
Call toll-free! **800-929-2929** 7 am-12 midnight

BK

Or fax your order to 802-864-7627
For fastest service order online:
www.bkconnection.com

Put the leading-edge business practices you read about to use in your work and in your organization.

DO YOU EVER wish there was a forum in your organization for discussing the newest trends and ideas in the business world? Do you wish you could explore the leading-edge business practices you read about with others in your company? Do you wish you could set aside a few hours every month to connect with like-minded coworkers or to get to know others in your business community?

If you answered yes to any of these questions, then the answer is simple: Start a business book reading group in your organization or business community. For step-by-step advice on how to do just that, visit the Berrett-Koehler website at <www.bkconnection.com> and click on "Reading Groups." There you'll find specific guidelines to help in all aspects of creating a successful reading group—from locating interested participants to selecting books, and facilitating discussions.

Berrett-Koehler is dedicated to providing you with tools to help you build a dialog with others in your company or business community, share ideas, build lasting relationships, and bring new ideas and knowledge to bear in your work and organizations.

For more information on how to start a business book reading group, or to browse or download the study guides that are available for our books, please visit our website at www.bkconnection.com.

Berrett-Koehler Publishers
PO Box 565, Williston, VT 05495-9900
Call toll-free! **800-929-2929** 7 am-12 midnight
Or fax your order to 802-864-7627
For fastest service order online:
www.bkconnection.com